4/00

Palo Alto City Library

South Africa

Mary N. Oluonye

🌿 Carolrhoda Books, Inc. / Minneapolis

Photo Acknowledgments

Photos, maps, and artworks are used courtesy of: John Erste, pp. 1, 2–3, 22–23, 24, 29, 39, 42–43; Laura Westlund, pp. 4–5, 19; South African Tourism Board, pp. 6 (left) 7 (bottom), 8 (top), 10, 18–19 (top), 21, 22 (right), 23, 33; © Trip/L. Reemer, pp. 6–7 (top), 8 (bottom); © Jason Laure, pp. 9, 13 (bottom), 17 (bottom), 19 (bottom), 20 (bottom), 31 (bottom), 34 (left), 37, 40, 41, 42 (bottom), 42–43 (top), 44; ©Trip/S. Harris, pp. 11, 14 (left), 15, 17 (top), 22 (left), 29, 31 (top), 32 (top), 43 (bottom); © Trip/B. Mnguni, p. 12; © Trip/M. Peters, p. 13 (top); © Trip/F. Nichols, p. 14 (right); © Trip/D. Saunders, pp. 16 (bottom), 28 (right); © Trip/D. Butcher, pp. 20 (top), 32 (bottom), 34 (right); © Trip/F. Torrance, p. 25; © Trip/W. Jacobs, p. 26; © Elaine Little/World Photo Images, pp. 27, 28 (left); © Trip/TH-Foto Werbung, p. 30; © Trip/J. Turco, p. 36 (top); © Trip/D. Burrows, p. 36 (bottom); © Trip/Hopalong Productions, p. 38; © Trip/A. Tovy, p. 45. Cover photo of mother and son © Trip/D. Saunders.

Carolrhoda Books, Inc.
A Division of the Lerner Publishing Group
241 First Avenue North
Minneapolis, Minnesota 55401 U.S.A.

Website address: www.lernerbooks.com

Library of Congress Cataloging-in-Publication Data

Oluonye, Mary N.
    South Africa / by Mary N. Oluonye.
      p.   cm. – (A ticket to)
    Includes index.
    Summary: Describes the people, government, geography, religion, language, customs, lifestyle, and culture of South Africa.
      ISBN 1-57505-141-9 (lib. bdg. : alk. paper)
      1. South Africa—Juvenile literature. [1. South Africa.]
    I. Title. II. Series.
    DT1719.0484   1999
    968—dc21   98–54223

Manufactured in the United States of America
1 2 3 4 5 6 – JR – 04 03 02 01 00 99

Contents

South Africa sits at the southernmost tip of the African **continent.** The Atlantic Ocean washes South Africa's west coast. The Indian Ocean touches beaches in the east and the south. South Africa's northern side meets Namibia, Botswana, Zimbabwe, Mozambique, and Swaziland.

And the tiny country of Lesotho is tucked into eastern South Africa.

The Land

The highest mountains in the Drakensberg range (left) *reach 11,000 feet. Sand dunes rise in the Namib Desert* (above).

Most of South Africa is dry and sunny. In the northwest, the Namib **Desert** crosses into South Africa from Namibia. In the east, thick green forests, hills, and valleys take over. Farther inland, tall mountains can be found in the Drakensberg range. The flat and

grassy middle part of the country is called the veld. That is Dutch for "field."

The Kalahari Desert is located in the northern part of South Africa.

Map Whiz Quiz

Take a look at the map on pages 4 and 5. Trace the outline of South Africa onto a piece of paper. Look for Botswana. Mark that with an "N" for north. See the Atlantic Ocean? Mark that with a "W" for west. Now find the Indian Ocean. It gets an "E" for east. Find the Cape of Good Hope. Below it, write an "S" for south. Then use an orange crayon to color in South Africa.

Finding Water

In a sunny country like South Africa, water dries up fast.

The Orange River (left) begins in Lesotho and flows westward until it empties into the Atlantic Ocean. Splash! Robeni Falls (above) is just one of the many waterfalls found in eastern South Africa.

The many short rivers that do cross the land are shallow. Sometimes they are filled with sand instead of water! The three main rivers are the Orange, the Vaal, and the Limpopo. The Orange River is the longest.

In Hot Water

Currents make the waves that roll into the Cape of Good Hope feel ice-cold.

The beaches along the eastern coast near Durban are the place to play. This coast enjoys the warm Agulhas Current that travels southward from the central Indian Ocean. On the western coast, though, the waters of the Atlantic Ocean can be pretty cold. That is because the cold Benguela Current flows north from icy Antarctica. Brrrr!

A Khoisan artist drew this buffalo on a cave wall.

First Folks

For a long time, only black people lived in South Africa. These people were from the Khoisan **ethnic group.**

Hundreds of years ago, Bantu-speaking peoples arrived in present-day South Africa from lands farther north. Many different groups spoke Bantu languages, including the Zulu and the Xhosa. The Bantu-speakers

Old Homes

In the past, traditional Zulu homes were round buildings made of tightly woven grasses. The door was low to the ground, so people had to bend down to go inside. The right half of the house was for men, and the left half was for women. In the back of the house, Zulu families stored food, pots, and pans. The homes in a traditional Zulu kraal (village) formed a large circle.

Long ago the Khoisan raised cattle near the Cape of Good Hope.

pushed the Khoisan south and west to the modern-day city of Cape Town. The Bantu-speakers stayed in what came to be known as KwaZulu-Natal.

People

People of many ethnic groups live in South Africa. Black South Africans make up most of the population. The Zulu and the Xhosa are the two largest groups.

All dressed up! These two South Africans (left) *are members of the Kwandebele ethnic group. An Afrikaner family* (facing page, bottom)

Some white South Africans speak English. Their **ancestors** came from Great Britain. Others are Afrikaners and speak

These Xhosa kids chill out.

Afrikaans, a language based on Dutch. They came to South Africa from Europe. Coloured South Africans mix black, white, and Asian backgrounds.

Apartheid laws forced many South Africans to move (left). Signs like this one (below) kept ethnic groups separated.

NET NIE BLANKES
NON-WHITES ONLY

Apartheid

For almost 40 years, the South African government made sure people followed a set of rules called **apartheid.** Apartheid separated the country's ethnic groups.

White South Africans controlled the government and made sure that whites got the best of everything. People of different groups had to live in separate areas and go to different schools. In 1990 South Africa ended the apartheid laws. In 1994 Nelson Mandela, a black man, was elected president of South Africa.

Former president F.W. de Klerk and new president Nelson Mandela (right) *joined hands in 1994.*

Going Home

Where do you live? Half of all black South Africans have homes in neighborhoods called townships. Soweto is the biggest. The houses in townships are small and crowded together.

Take a look inside of this house in a South African township.

This township home (left) sits in Soweto. A birthday party in the backyard of a white family's home (below)

Many township kids have to haul water from wells back to their homes.
Most Coloured South Africans live in Cape Town. Many Asian South Africans like the city of Durban best. Durban has great beaches. Lots of white South Africans live close to big cities. Many of their homes are new, large, and roomy.

City Life

Check it out! South Africa's big cities have high-rise buildings, shopping malls, and parks. Johannesburg, sometimes called Jo'burg, is South Africa's biggest city. Jo'burg sprang up in the late 1800s after a couple of kids stumbled upon rocks that could be made into diamonds.

Some call Cape Town one of the most beautiful cities in the whole world. It faces

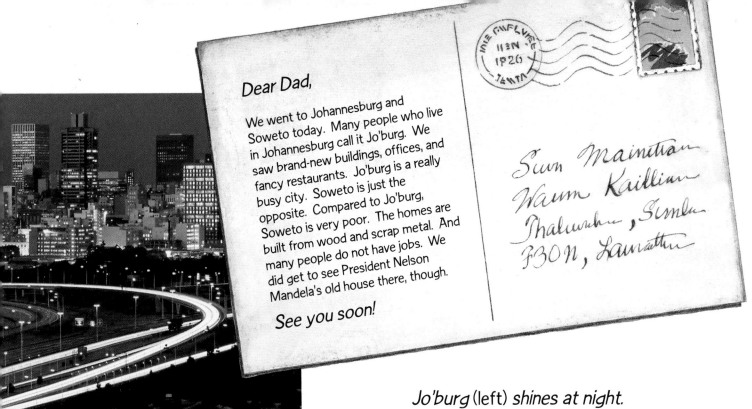

Dear Dad,

We went to Johannesburg and Soweto today. Many people who live in Johannesburg call it Jo'burg. We saw brand-new buildings, offices, and fancy restaurants. Jo'burg is a really busy city. Soweto is just the opposite. Compared to Jo'burg, Soweto is very poor. The homes are built from wood and scrap metal. And many people do not have jobs. We did get to see President Nelson Mandela's old house there, though.

See you soon!

Jo'burg (left) *shines at night. Cape Town* (below) *is South Africa's oldest city.*

the Atlantic Ocean and sits at the bottom of Table Mountain. Clouds sometimes hide the top of the mountain.

On the Go

Beep, beep! South African highways make travel easy for people with cars. In cities people get around in taxis or

What a nifty way to go! Tourists in Durban ride on a tuk tuk (above). Get in line! That is what South Africans who travel by minibus (left) do at the end of the workday.

Some tourists come to South Africa just to ride the fancy Blue Train. It snakes through beautiful countryside as it chugs from Pretoria to Cape Town. All aboard!

minibuses. Minibuses are the cheapest way to go. But be careful! Many minibus drivers speed along roads and sometimes go right through red lights.

For fun in the city, take a ride on a tuk tuk. A tuk tuk is a two-wheeled or four-wheeled cart that is pulled by a driver on foot.

This elephant (left) *calls Kruger National Park home. Two springboks* (above) *drink up.*

Animal Tracks

Wow! Talk about some BIG animals! People go to Kruger National Park hoping to see the big five—elephants, lions, leopards, buffalo, and rhinos. Folks might also find giraffes or even the springbok antelope, South Africa's national animal. Keep in mind that a trip to

Kruger is much better than going to the city zoo. Visitors can watch the animals in their natural homes. Pretty neat!

Take a Hike!

There are lots of good places to hike in South Africa. Some hiking trails are very easy and take one or two hours to finish. But on other trails, you can expect to walk for several days. Whew! On such a long trip, there may be huts or caves for hikers to sleep in during the night. There is nothing to be afraid of, though. People do it all the time.

The protea is South Africa's national flower.

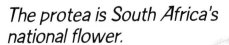

Time to Talk

How many languages do you speak? Most South Africans can speak two or even three languages! In South Africa, there are as many as 32 different languages and **dialects.** Really! South Africans speak Afrikaans more than any of the other languages. Afrikaans,

Hippo crossing? This sign is printed in Afrikaans and English.

GEVAARLIK   SNAGS

DANGEROUS AT NIGHT

spoken only in South Africa, is based on Dutch. But it also has words from English, German, French, Malay, Portuguese, and black South African languages. Afrikaners and Coloured South Africans speak Afrikaans.

In English

Many black South Africans speak English, because that is the language they learn in school. When talking to black friends, black South Africans like to speak their own local language. It might be Zulu, Ndebele, Swati, or Tsonga.

Families

A South African family poses for a picture outside their Soweto home.

South African families are close. Country kids tend to live with their brothers, sisters, parents, grandparents, and sometimes aunts, uncles, and cousins. In the cities, children usually live with just their parents, brothers, and sisters.

During apartheid many black men had to find work far away from their families. When apartheid ended, black families were together again.

All in the Family

Here are the Afrikaans words for family members. Try them out on your own family.

grandfather	*oupa*	OH-pah
grandmother	*ouma*	OH-mah
father	*fader*	FAH-der
mother	*moeder*	MOH-der
uncle	*oom*	OO-wem
aunt	*tante*	THANT
son	*seun*	SEE-en
daughter	*dogter*	DOG-ter
brother	*broer*	BREW-er
sister	*suster*	SUS-ter

Kids in Johannesburg line up after recess (left). Even in uniform (above), some South African kids just like to be goofy.

School

Brrring! The bell rings at 8:00 A.M. to begin the schoolday. For the first few years, South African students learn in the language of their ethnic group. Later they will study English and Afrikaans. All South African kids take science, geography, math, religion, and home economics classes. At 2:00 P.M. another bell rings. School is out!

How It Works

South African kids start grade one at age seven. After grade two, classes are called standards. Instead of saying that they are in grade three, kids say they are in standard one. At the end of standard five, students go to high school for five years. After high school, kids take a big test. Colleges look at these tests to decide who to admit to their schools. What a nail-biter!

Study hard! These Soweto students try to do well in school.

29

Religions

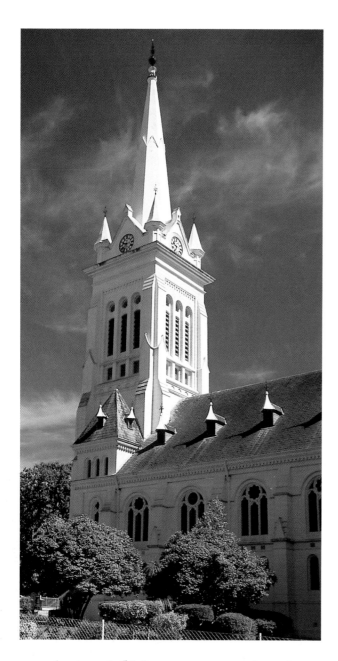

Lots of Afrikaners go to churches like this Dutch Reformed church.

Traditional African religion is the oldest of all South African faiths. Followers believe in a Supreme Being who created the world. But spirits, especially those of ancestors, are very important. Spirits help believers every day.

European settlers brought Christianity and Judaism. Most South Africans are Christians who belong to the Dutch Reformed Church.

This traditional healer (above) plays a big part in traditional African religious ceremonies. He shops for herbs to heal the sick. (Right) Folks who go to church in South Africa love to sing. Do you?

Celebrate!

Put on your party hat! South Africans have lots to celebrate. On

Christmas decorations light up Johannesburg's streets during the holidays.

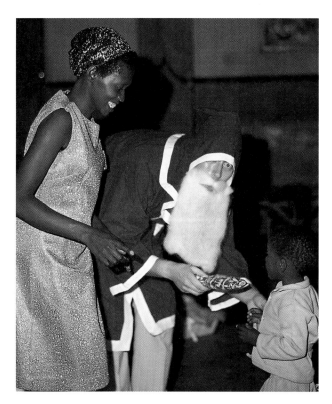

Father Christmas makes the rounds on Christmas Day.

Christmas Eve, South African kids leave their pillows at the foot of their beds. During the night, Father

Christmas sneaks in and fills the pillowcases with goodies. What fun!

Grahamstown Festival

South Africa holds many celebrations throughout the year. Thousands go to the biggest event—the Grahamstown Festival—in July. Costumed performers stroll through the streets, and artists sell their work at booths. People gather around to listen to writers and poets read out loud. Traditional, ballet, and Indian dancers entertain audiences. There is music of all kinds to listen to and enjoy.

Now you are cooking! Afrikaners (left) love to cook meat on a grill. Yum! There is nothing like a hot plate of mealies (above) covered in gravy.

Time to Eat

In South Africa, there is plenty of tasty meat, seafood, fruits, and vegetables to munch on. If you like corn, you will love traditional African cooking. Mealies is corn cooked into a smooth porridge and eaten with a flavor-packed stew made from vegetables, meat, and spices. Recipes brought to South Africa from Germany and the Netherlands are an important part of Afrikaner cooking. Big favorites are homemade *boerwors* (spicy sausages), steak, and fish. These meats can be cooked over an open fire on a grill called a *braai*.

CHOMP
CRUNCH
CHOMP

A New Kind of Sandwich

In the mood for fast food? Instead of a hamburger, try a bunny chow. Bunny chow is a popular Asian South African fast food. It is made from a loaf of bread cut in half. The middle of the loaf is scooped out and stuffed with beans, chicken, fish, or vegetables. Sounds tasty!

Art

In mountain caves, Khoisan people drew scenes from their everyday lives. These pictures of people, animals,

Visitors to Johannesburg's Museum of Rock Art might see this piece (left). *These masks* (above) *would be great for Halloween, right? The masks peep from behind grass baskets at a market.*

hunting, and battles are called rock art. Visitors tour caves near the Drakensberg Mountains to see the rock paintings up close.

Zulu women create another kind of art. They weave baskets from grasses or other plant parts. Some baskets are woven so tightly that you can fill them with water and they will not leak a single drop!

Many tourists visit African cultural villages to learn about traditional African crafts.

It looks as if these kids are enjoying the story.

Tell a Story

A great South African children's story was told by actors on stage, not in the pages of a book. The play *Sarafina!* by Mbondgeni Ngema is about the Soweto Uprising. In 1976 people filled Soweto's streets to **protest** a law that made black kids study

Afrikaans. Many were hurt or killed when police fired into the crowd.

The Maiden of the River

Long ago there was a father who had two daughters named Nomkhosi and Somate. The father loved Somate so much that there was no love left over for Nomkhosi. But Somate's love for her sister made the father jealous. One day he took Nomkhosi to the river and threw her in to drown. But a snake named Monya gently wrapped his giant coils around Nomkhosi and cast a spell on her with his eyes. Nomkhosi then lived in the river.

Months later Somate saw her lost sister in the river. Somate begged Nomkhosi to come home, but Nomkhosi was happy where she was. Somate kept it secret for a long time, but one day she was so sad she told her father. The father went to the river and told Nomkhosi to come home. When Monya found out, he made the river rise into big waves. Monya rode the waves into shore. He entered Nomkhosi's house and carried her back into the river. To this day, Nomkhosi lives happily with her friends in the river.

Gum boot dancing began in South Africa's gold mines. Stomp your feet!

Music

Music lovers in South Africa have lots of different styles to choose from. You may have heard of Ladysmith Black Mombaza, a South African musical group that has sung on Sesame Street. The group sings traditional music that started in the gold mines of South Africa. Most of the time, they sing a capella—that means without the help of musical instruments. Ladysmith Black Mombaza's Zulu songs are about peace and love.

Traditional Tunes

Take a trip to a rural village and you will hear traditional black South African music. Musicians play the drums, xylophones,  and flutelike instruments called *agamfes*. The high-pitched, happy sound of whistles, called *impempes*, comes in short bursts throughout the music.

Play Time

Soweto's playgrounds are a fun place to play.

On weekends, many South African families head to the beach to swim and to enjoy the sun. South Africans also like soccer and rugby (a British

Soccer on the beach? Sure! Just make sure a wave does not steal the ball (left). Folks relax at a Durban beach (below).

game similar to American football.) In many black neighborhoods, boys and girls kick a ball around on a soccer field. What do you like to do?

Ndebele artists use bright colors to paint these leather bracelets and belts.

New Words to Learn

ancestor: A person from whom others are descended.

apartheid: Laws that were designed to separate ethnic groups in South Africa and to give special privileges to whites.

continent: Any one of seven large areas of land. A few of the continents are Africa, Asia, and North America.

desert: A dry and often sandy region.

dialect: A type of language that is set apart by vocabulary, grammar, and pronunciation from other varieties of the same language.

ethnic group: A group of people with many things in common, such as language, religion, and customs.

Whee! Cable cars run from Cape Town to the top of Table Mountain.

protest: To object, using words or gestures, to an idea or action.

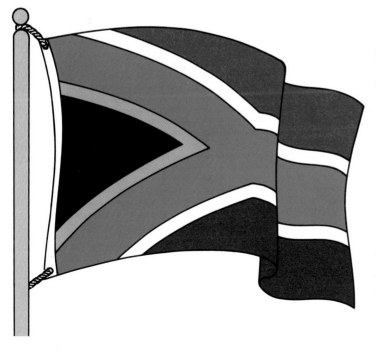

South Africa raised this new flag in 1994 when apartheid ended.

New Words to Say

Afrikaans	ah-free-KAHNS
agamfes	ah-GUM-fehs
Agulhas	ah-GUH-lahs
apartheid	ah-PART-hate
Benguela	ben-GWEH-lah
boerwors	boo-reh-VORS
braai	BREYE
impempes	im-PEMP-ehs
Khoisan	koy-SAN
kraal	KRAWL
KwaZulu-Natal	kwah-ZOO-loo—neh-TULL
Mbondgeni Ngema	um-BON-jen-ee en-GEH-mah
mealies	MEE-leez
Ndebele	en-duh-BEH-leh
Nguni	en-GUH-nee
Soweto	so-WEH-toh
Tsonga	TSON-gah
Xhosa	KOH-zah
Zulu	ZOO-loo

More Books to Read

Cornell, Christine. *The Zulu of Southern Africa.* New York: Power Kids Press, 1996.

Dell, Pamela. *Nelson Mandela: Freedom for South Africa.* Chicago: Children's Press, 1994.

Haskins, Jim. *Count Your Way Through Africa.* Minneapolis: Carolrhoda Books, Inc., 1989.

Heinrichs, Ann. *South Africa.* New York: Children's Press, 1997.

Lewin, Hugh. *Jafta* series. Minneapolis: Carolrhoda Books, Inc., 1983–1984.

Nabwire, Constance and Bertha Vining Montgomery. *Cooking the African Way.* Minneapolis: Lerner Publications Company, 1988.

Sisulu, Elinor Batezat. *The Day Gogo Went to Vote: South Africa.* 1994. Boston: Little Brown & Company, 1996.

Smith, Roland. *African Elephants.* Minneapolis: Lerner Publications, 1995.

Stewart, Dianne. *Gift of the Sun: A Tale from South Africa.* New York: Farrar Straus & Giroux, 1996.

Temko, Florence. *Traditional Crafts from Africa.* Minneapolis: Lerner Publications Company, 1996.

Walker, Sally M. *Rhinos.* Minneapolis: Carolrhoda Books, Inc., 1996.

New Words to Find